Intermittent Fasting Guide And Cookbook

INTERMITTENT FAST VERY EASY FOR BEGINNERS, RECIPE IDEAS AND HEALTHY NUTRITION PLAN, PERMANENT WEIGHT LOSS WITHOUT CALORIE COUNTING.

Table of Contents

—

BREAKFAST RECIPES

Cheese Omelet

Preparation Time: 5 minutes

Cooking Time: 10 minutes

Servings: 2

Ingredients:

- 6 eggs

- 3 ozs. ghee

- 7 ozs. shredded cheddar cheese

- salt and pepper

Directions:

1. Whisk the eggs until smooth. Compound half of the cheese and season it with salt and pepper.

2. Melt the butter in a pan. Pour in the mixture and let it sit for a few minutes (3-4)

3. When the mixture is looking good, add the other half of the cheese. Serve immediately.

Nutrition: Carbs: 4 g Fat: 80 g Protein: 40 g Calories: 897 kcal

Capicola Egg Cups

Preparation Time: 5 minutes

Cooking Time: 15 minutes

Servings: 4

Ingredients:

- 8 eggs

- 1 cup cheddar cheese

- 4 oz. capicola or bacon (slices)

- salt, pepper, basil

Directions:

1. Preheat the oven to 400°F. You will need 8 wells of a standard-size muffin pan.

2. Place the slices in the 8 wells, forming a cup shape. Sprinkle into each cup some of the cheese, according to your liking.

3. Crack an egg into each cup, season them with salt and pepper.

4. Bake for 10-15 mins. Serve hot, top it with basil.

Nutrition: Carbs: 1 g Fat: 11 g Protein: 16 g Calories: 171 kcal

Overnight "noats"

Preparation Time: 5 minutes plus overnight to chill

Cooking Time: 10 minutes

Servings: 1

Ingredients:

- 2 tablespoons hulled hemp seeds
- 1 tablespoon chia seeds
- ½ scoop (about 8 grams) collagen powder
- ½ cup unsweetened nut or seed milk (hemp, almond, coconut, and cashew)

Direction:

1. In a small mason jar or glass container, combine the hemp seeds, chia seeds, collagen, and milk.
2. Secure tightly with a lid, shake well, and refrigerate overnight.

Nutrition: Calories: 263 Total Fat: 19g Protein: 16g Total Carbs: 7g Fiber: 5g Net Carbs: 2g

Frozen intermittent coffee

Preparation Time: 5 minutes

Cooking Time: 20 minutes

Servings: 1

Ingredients:

- 12 ounces coffee, chilled

- 1 scoop MCT powder (or 1 tablespoon MCT oil)

- 1 tablespoon heavy (whipping) cream

- Pinch ground cinnamon

- Dash sweetener (optional)

- ½ cup ice

Directions:

1. In a blender, combine the coffee, MCT powder, cream, cinnamon, sweetener (if using), and ice. Blend until smooth.

Nutrition: Calories: 127; Total Fat: 13g; Protein: 1g; Total Carbs: 1.5g; Fiber: 1g; Net Carbs: 0.5g

Easy Skillet Pancakes

Preparation Time: 5 minutes

Cooking Time: 5 minutes

Servings: 8

Ingredients:

- 8 ounces cream cheese

- 8 eggs

- 2 tablespoons coconut flour

- 2 teaspoons baking powder

- 1 teaspoon ground cinnamon

- ½ teaspoon vanilla extract

- 1 teaspoon liquid stevia or sweetener of choice (optional)

- 2 tablespoons butter

Directions

1. In a blender, combine the cream cheese, eggs, coconut flour, baking powder, cinnamon, vanilla, and stevia (if using). Blend until smooth.

2. In a large skillet over medium heat, melt the butter.

3. Use half the mixture to pour four evenly sized pancakes and cook for about a minute, until you see bubbles on top. Flip the pancakes and cook for another minute. Remove from the pan and add more butter or oil to the skillet if needed. Repeat with the remaining batter.

4. Top with butter and eat right away, or freeze the pancakes in a freezer-safe resealable bag with sheets of parchment in between, for up to 1 month.

Nutrition: Calories: 179 Total Fat: 15g Protein: 8g Total Carbs: 3g Fiber: 1g Net Carbs: 2g

Quick Intermittent Blender Muffins

Preparation Time: 5 minutes

Cooking Time: 25 minutes

Servings: 12

Ingredients

- Butter, ghee, or coconut oil for greasing the pan
- 6 eggs
- 8 ounces cream cheese, at room temperature
- 2 scoops flavored collagen powder
- 1 teaspoon ground cinnamon
- 1 teaspoon baking powder
- Few drops or dash sweetener (optional)

Directions:

1. Preheat the oven to 350°F. Grease a 12-cup muffin pan very well with butter, ghee, or coconut oil. Alternatively, you can use silicone cups or paper muffin liners.

2. In a blender, combine the eggs, cream cheese, collagen powder, cinnamon, baking powder, and sweetener (if using). Blend until well combined and pour the mixture into the muffin cups, dividing equally.

3. Bake for 22 to 25 minutes until the muffins are golden brown on top and firm.

4. Let cool then store in a glass container or plastic bag in the refrigerator for up to 2 weeks or in the freezer for up to 3 months.

5. To Servings refrigerated muffins, heat in the microwave for 30 seconds. To Servings from frozen, thaw in the refrigerator overnight and then microwave for 30 seconds, or microwave straight from the freezer for 45 to 60 seconds or until heated through.

Nutrition: Calories: 120 Total Fat: 10g Protein: 6g Total Carbs: 1.5g Fiber: 0g Net Carbs: 1.5g

Intermittent Everything Bagels

Preparation Time: 10 minutes

Cooking Time: 15 minutes

Servings: 8

Ingredients:

- 2 cups shredded mozzarella cheese
- 2 tablespoons labneh cheese (or cream cheese)
- 1½ cups almond flour
- 1 egg
- 2 teaspoons baking powder
- ¼ teaspoon sea salt
- 1 tablespoon

Directions

1. Preheat the oven to 400°F.

2. In a microwave-safe bowl, combine the mozzarella and labneh cheeses. Microwave for 30 seconds, stir, then microwave for another 30 seconds. Stir well. If not melted completely, microwave for another 10 to 20 seconds.

3. Add the almond flour, egg, baking powder, and salt to the bowl and mix well. Form into a dough using a spatula or your hands.

4. Cut the dough into 8 roughly equal pieces and form into balls.

5. Roll each dough ball into a cylinder, then pinch the ends together to seal.

6. Place the dough rings in a nonstick donut pan or arrange them on a parchment paper–lined baking sheet.

7. Sprinkle with the seasoning and bake for 12 to 15 minutes or until golden brown.

8. Store in plastic bags in the freezer and defrost overnight in the refrigerator. Reheat in the oven or toaster for a quick grab-and-go breakfast.

Nutrition: Calories: 241 Total Fat: 19g Protein: 12g Total Carbs: 5.5g Fiber: 2.5g Net Carbs: 3g

Turmeric Chicken and Kale Salad with Food, Lemon and Honey

Preparation Time: 20 minutes

Cooking Time: 15 minutes

Servings: 4

Ingredients:

- For the chicken:

- 1 teaspoon of clarified butter or 1 tablespoon of coconut oil

- ½ medium brown onion, diced

- 250-300 g / 9 ounces minced chicken meat or diced chicken legs

- 1 large garlic clove, diced

- 1 teaspoon of turmeric powder

- 1 teaspoon of lime zest

- ½ lime juice

- ½ teaspoon of salt + pepper

- For the salad:

- 6 stalks of broccoli or 2 cups of broccoli flowers

- 2 tablespoons of pumpkin seeds (seeds)

- 3 large cabbage leaves, stems removed and chopped

- ½ sliced avocado

- Handful of fresh coriander leaves, chopped

- Handful of fresh parsley leaves, chopped

- For the dressing:

- 3 tablespoons of lime juice

- 1 small garlic clove, diced or grated

- 3 tablespoons of virgin olive oil (I used 1 tablespoon of avocado oil and 2 tablespoons of EVO)

- 1 teaspoon of raw honey

- ½ teaspoon whole or Dijon mustard

- ½ teaspoon of sea salt with pepper

Directions:

1. Heat the coconut oil in a pan. Add the onion and sauté over medium heat for 4-5 minutes, until golden brown. Add the minced chicken and garlic and stir 2-3 minutes over medium-high heat, separating.

2. Add your turmeric, lime zest, lime juice, salt and pepper, and cook, stirring consistently, for another 3-4 minutes. Set the ground beef aside.

3. While your chicken is cooking, put a small saucepan of water to the boil. Add your broccoli and cook for 2 minutes. Rinse with cold water and cut into 3-4 pieces each.

4. Add the pumpkin seeds to the chicken pan and toast over medium heat for 2 minutes, frequently stirring to avoid

burning. Season with a little salt. Set aside. Raw pumpkin seeds are also good to use.

5. Put the chopped cabbage in a salad bowl and pour it over the dressing. Using your hands, mix, and massage the cabbage with the dressing. This will soften the cabbage, a bit like citrus juice with fish or beef Carpaccio: its "cooks" it a little.

6. Finally, mix the cooked chicken, broccoli, fresh herbs, pumpkin seeds, and avocado slices.

Nutrition: 232 calories Fat 11 Fiber 9 Carbs 8 Protein 14

LUNCH RECIPES

Bacon Cheeseburger

Preparation Time: 15 minutes

Cooking Time: 30 minutes

Servings: 12

Ingredients:

- Low-sodium bacon (16 oz. pkg.)
- Ground beef (3 lb.)
- Eggs (2)
- Medium chopped onion (half of 1)
- Shredded cheddar cheese (8 oz.)

Directions:

1. Fry the bacon and chop it to bits. Shred the cheese and dice the onion.
2. Combine the mixture with the beef and blend in the whisked eggs.
3. Prepare 24 burgers and grill them the way you like them.
4. You can make a double-decker since they are small.
5. If you like a bigger burger, you can make 12 burgers as a single-decker.

Nutrition: Net Carbohydrates: 0.8 grams Protein Counts: 27 grams Total Fats: 41 grams Calories: 489

Cauliflower Mac & Cheese

Preparation Time: 15 minutes

Cooking Time: 20 minutes

Servings: 4

Ingredients:

- Cauliflower (1 head)
- Butter (3 tbsp.)
- Unsweetened almond milk (.25 cup)
- Heavy cream (.25 cup)
- Cheddar cheese (1 cup)

Directions:

1. Use a sharp knife to slice the cauliflower into small florets. Shred the cheese. Prepare the oven to reach 450° Fahrenheit. Cover a baking pan with a layer of parchment baking paper or foil.
2. Add two tablespoons of the butter to a pan and melt. Add the florets, butter, salt, and pepper together. Place the cauliflower on the baking pan and roast 10 to 15 minutes.
3. Warm up the rest of the butter, milk, heavy cream, and cheese in the microwave or double boiler. Pour the cheese over the cauliflower and serve.

Nutrition: Net Carbohydrates: 7 grams Protein Counts: 11 grams Total Fats: 23 grams Calories: 294 grams

Mushroom & Cauliflower Risotto

Preparation Time: 5 minutes

Cooking Time: 10 minutes

Servings: 4

Ingredients:

- Grated head of cauliflower (1)
- Vegetable stock (1 cup)
- Chopped mushrooms (9 oz.)
- Butter (2 tbsp.)
- Coconut cream (1 cup)

Directions:

1. Pour the stock in a saucepan. Boil and set aside. Prepare a skillet with butter and sauté the mushrooms until golden.
2. Grate and stir in the cauliflower and stock. Simmer and add the cream, cooking until the cauliflower is al dente. Serve.

Nutrition: Net Carbohydrates: 4 grams Protein Counts: 1 gram Total Fats: 17 grams Calories: 186

Pita Pizza

Preparation Time: 15 minutes

Cooking Time: 10 minutes

Servings: 2

Ingredients:

- Marinara sauce (.5 cup)
- Low-carb pita (1)
- Cheddar cheese (2 oz.)
- Pepperoni (14 slices)
- Roasted red peppers (1 oz.)

Directions:

1. Program the oven temperature setting to 450° Fahrenheit.
2. Slice the pita in half and place onto a foil-lined baking tray. Rub with a bit of oil and toast for one to two minutes.
3. Pour the sauce over the bread. Sprinkle using the cheese and other toppings. Bake until the cheese melts (5 min.). Cool thoroughly.

Nutrition: Net Carbohydrates: 4 grams Protein Counts: 13 grams Total Fats: 19 grams Calories: 250

Skillet Cabbage Tacos

Preparation Time: 10 minutes

Cooking Time: 15 minutes

Servings: 4

Ingredients:

- Ground beef (1 lb.)
- Salsa - ex. Pace Organic (.5 cup)
- Shredded cabbage (2 cups)
- Chili powder (2 tsp.)
- Shredded cheese (.75 cup)

Directions:

1. Brown the beef and drain the fat. Pour in the salsa, cabbage, and seasoning.
2. Cover and lower the heat. Simmer for 10 to 12 minutes using the medium heat temperature setting.
3. When the cabbage has softened, remove it from the heat and mix in the cheese.
4. Top it off using your favorite toppings, such as green onions or sour cream, and serve.

Nutrition: Net Carbohydrates: 4 grams Protein Counts: 30 grams Total Fats: 21 grams Calories: 325

Taco Casserole

Preparation Time: 10 minutes

Cooking Time: 20 minutes

Servings: 8

Ingredients:

- Ground turkey or beef (1.5 to 2 lb.)
- Taco seasoning (2 tbsp.) Shredded cheddar cheese (8 oz.)
- Salsa (1 cup) Cottage cheese (16 oz.)

Directions:

1. Heat the oven to reach 400° Fahrenheit.
2. Combine the taco seasoning and ground meat in a casserole dish. Bake it for 20 minutes.
3. Combine the salsa and both kinds of cheese. Set aside for now.
4. Carefully transfer the casserole dish from the oven. Drain away the cooking juices from the meat.
5. Break the meat into small pieces and mash with a potato masher or fork.
6. Sprinkle with cheese. Bake in the oven for 15 to 20 more minutes until the top is browned.

Nutrition: Net Carbohydrates: 6 grams Protein Counts: 45 grams Total Fats: 18 grams Calories: 367

Creamy Chicken Salad

Preparation Time: 10 minutes

Cooking Time: 30 minutes

Servings: 4

Ingredients:

- Chicken Breast - 1 Lb.
- Avocado - 2
- Garlic Cloves - 2,
- Minced Lime Juice - 3 T.
- Onion - .33 C.,
- Minced Jalapeno Pepper - 1,
- Minced Salt - Dash Cilantro - 1 T.
- Pepper - Dash

Directions

1. You will want to start this recipe off my prepping the stove to 400. As this warms up, get out your cooking sheet and line it with paper or foil.
2. Next, it is time to get out the chicken.
3. Go ahead and layer the chicken breast up with some olive oil before seasoning to your liking.
4. When the chicken is all set, you will want to line them along the surface of your cooking sheet and pop it into the oven for about twenty minutes.
5. By the end of twenty minutes, the chicken should be cooked through and can be taken out of the oven for chilling.
6. Once cool enough to handle, you will want to either dice or shred your chicken, dependent upon how you like your chicken salad.

7. Now that your chicken is all cooked, it is time to assemble your salad!
8. You can begin this process by adding everything into a bowl and mashing down the avocado.
9. Once your ingredients are mended to your liking, sprinkle some salt over the top and serve immediately.

Nutrition: Fats: 20g Carbs: 4g Proteins: 25g

Spicy Intermittent Chicken Wings

Preparation Time: 20 minutes

Cooking Time: 30 minutes

Servings: 4

Ingredients:

- Chicken Wings - 2 Lbs.
- Cajun Spice - 1 t.
- Smoked Paprika - 2 t.
- Turmeric - .50 t.
- Salt - Dash
- Baking Powder - 2 t.
- Pepper - Dash

Directions:

1. When you first begin the Diet, you may find that you won't be eating the traditional foods that may have made up a majority of your diet in the past.
2. While this is a good thing for your health, you may feel you are missing out! The good news is that there are delicious alternatives that aren't lacking in flavor! To start this recipe, you'll want to prep the stove to 400.
3. As this heats up, you will want to take some time to dry your chicken wings with a paper towel. This will help remove any excess moisture and get you some nice, crispy wings!
4. When you are all set, take out a mixing bowl and place all of the seasonings along with the baking powder. If you feel like it, you can adjust the seasoning levels however you would like.

5. Once these are set, go ahead and throw the chicken wings in and coat evenly. If you have one, you'll want to place the wings on a wire rack that is placed over your baking tray. If not, you can just lay them across the baking sheet.
6. Now that your chicken wings are set, you are going to pop them into the stove for thirty minutes. By the end of this time, the tops of the wings should be crispy.
7. If they are, take them out from the oven and flip them so that you can bake the other side. You will want to cook these for an additional thirty minutes.
8. Finally, take the tray from the oven and allow to cool slightly before serving up your spiced intermittent wings. For additional flavor, serve with any of your favorite, intermittent-friendly dipping sauce.

Nutrition: Fats: 7g Carbs: 1g Proteins: 60g

Cheesy Ham Quiche

Preparation Time: 10 minutes

Cooking Time: 30 minutes

Servings: 6

Ingredients:

- Eggs - 8
- Zucchini - 1 C.,
- Shredded heavy Cream - .50 C.
- Ham - 1 C., Diced
- Mustard - 1 t.
- Salt – Dash

Directions:

1. For this recipe, you can start off by prepping your stove to 375 and getting out a pie plate for your quiche.
2. Next, it is time to prep the zucchini. First, you will want to go ahead and shred it into small pieces.
3. Once this is complete, take a paper towel and gently squeeze out the excess moisture. This will help avoid a soggy quiche.
4. When the step from above is complete, you will want to place the zucchini into your pie plate along with the cooked ham pieces and your cheese.
5. Once these items are in place, you will want to whisk the seasonings, cream, and eggs together before pouring it over the top.
6. Now that your quiche is set, you are going to pop the dish into your stove for about forty minutes.

7. By the end of this time, the egg should be cooked through, and you will be able to insert a knife into the center and have it come out clean.
8. If the quiche is cooked to your liking, take the dish from the oven and allow it to chill slightly before slicing and serving.

Nutrition: Fats: 25g Carbs: 2g Proteins: 20g

Feta and Cauliflower Rice Stuffed Bell Peppers

Preparation Time: 10 minutes

Cooking Time: 20 minutes

Servings: 3

Ingredients:

- green Bell Pepper
- 1 red Bell Pepper
- 1 yellow Bell Pepper
- ½ cup Cauliflower rice
- 1 cup Feta cheese
- 1 Onion, sliced
- Tomatoes, chopped
- 1 tbsp black Pepper
- 2-3 Garlic clove, minced
- tbsp Lemon juice
- 3-4 green Olives, chopped
- 3-4 tbsp Olive oil
- Yogurt Sauce:
- 1 clove Garlic, pressed
- 1 cup Greek Yogurt
- kosher Salt, to taste
- juice from 1 Lemon
- 1 tbsp fresh Dill

Directions:

1. Grease the Instant Pot with olive oil. Make a cut at the top of the bell peppers near the stem. Place feta cheese, onion, olives, tomatoes, cauliflower rice, salt, black

pepper, garlic powder, and lemon juice into a bowl; mix well.

2. Fill up the bell peppers with the feta mixture and insert in the Instant Pot. Set on Manual and cook on High pressure for 20 minutes. When the timer beeps, allow the pressure to release naturally for 5 minutes, then do a quick pressure release.

3. To prepare the yogurt sauce, combine garlic, yogurt, lemon juice, salt, and fresh dill.

Nutrition: Calories 388, Protein 13.5g, Net Carbs 7.9g, Fat 32.4g

SIDE DISHES

Quick and Easy Mushroom Casserole

Preparation Time: 5 minutes

Cooking Time: 10 minutes

Servings: 4

Ingredients:

- 2 tablespoons olive oil
- 2 chicken breasts, boneless, skinless and cut into slices
- Sea salt, to taste
- 1/4 teaspoon ground black pepper
- 1/2 teaspoon cayenne pepper
- teaspoon fresh rosemary, finely minced
- pound Portobello mushrooms, sliced
- 1/2 cup scallions, chopped
- garlic cloves, minced
- teaspoon yellow mustard
- cup vegetable broth
- tablespoon Piri-Piri sauce

Directions:

1. Press the "Sauté" button to heat up your Instant Pot. Then, heat the oil. Cook the chicken until delicately browned on all sides.
2. Season with salt, black pepper, cayenne pepper, and rosemary; reserve.
3. Spritz the bottom and sides of your Instant Pot with a nonstick cooking spray. Add 1/2 of the mushrooms to the bottom.
4. Add a layer of chopped scallions and minced garlic. Add the chicken mixture. Top with the remaining mushrooms.
5. In a mixing bowl, thoroughly combine vegetable broth and Piri-Piri sauce. Pour this sauce into the Instant Pot.

---

6. Secure the lid. Choose "Manual" mode and High pressure; cook for 5 minutes. Once cooking is complete, use a quick pressure release; carefully remove the lid. Serve warm and enjoy!

Nutrition: 229 Calories; 10.6g Fat; 5.7g Total Carbs; 28.2g Protein; 2.6g Sugars

Easy Intermittent Steamed Salad

Preparation Time: 2 minutes

Cooking Time: 10 minutes

Servings: 4

Ingredients:

- cup water
- 8 tomatoes, sliced
- tablespoons extra-virgin olive oil
- 1/2 cup Halloumi cheese, crumbled
- garlic cloves, smashed
- 2 tablespoons fresh basil, snipped

Directions:

1. Add 1 cup of water and a steamer rack to the Instant Pot.
2. Place the tomatoes on the steamer rack.
3. Secure the lid. Choose "Manual" mode and High pressure; cook for 3 minutes. Once cooking is complete, use a quick pressure release; carefully remove the lid.
4. Toss the tomatoes with the remaining ingredients and serve. Enjoy!

Nutrition: 168 Calories; 12.4g Fat; 5.6g Total Carbs; 6.2g Protein; 3.5g Sugars

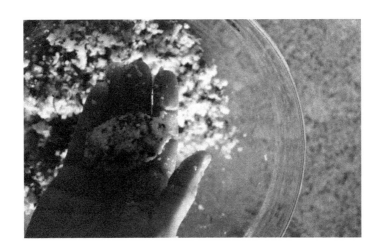

MEATS RECIPES

Lamb Burgers with Tzatziki

Preparation Time: 10 minutes

Cooking Time: 20 minutes

Servings: 4

Ingredients:

- lb. of grass-fed lamb
- ¼ cup chives finely chopped green onion or red onion if desired
- tbsp. chopped fresh dill
- ½ tsp dried oregano or about 1 tbsps. freshly chopped
- tbsp. finely chopped fresh mint
- A pinch of chopped red pepper
- Fine-grained sea salt
- tbsp. water
- tsp olive oil to grease the pan
- For the tzatziki
- can coconut milk with all the cooled fat and 1 tbsp. the discarded liquid portion **
- cloves of garlic
- peeled cucumber without seeds, roughly sliced
- tbsp. freshly squeezed lemon juice
- tbsp. chopped fresh dill
- 3/4 tsp fine grain sea salt
- Black pepper to taste

Directions:

1. To make the tzatziki:
2. Place the garlic, cucumber, and lemon juice in the food processor and press until finely chopped. Add the coconut cream, dill, salt, and pepper, and mix until well blended.
3. Put it in a jar with a lid and keep it in the refrigerator until it is served. The flavors become more intense over time when they cool in the fridge.
4. For burgers:
5. Thoroughly mix the ground lamb in a bowl with the chives or red onion, dill, oregano, mint, red pepper, and water.
6. Sprinkle the mixture with fine-grained sea salt and form 4 patties of the same size.
7. Heat a large cast-iron skillet over medium heat and brush with a small amount of olive oil. Lightly sprinkle the pan with fine-grain sea salt.
8. Bring the patties into the pan and cook on each side for about 4 min, adjusting the heat to prevent the outside from becoming too brown. Alternatively, you can grill the burgers.
9. Remove from the pan and cover with tzatziki sauce.

Nutrition: Calories: 363 kcal Protein: 35.33 g Fat: 22.14 g Carbohydrates: 6.83 g

Lamb Sliders

Preparation Time: 5 minutes

Cooking Time: 15 minutes

Servings: 6

Ingredients:

- lb. minced lamb or half veal, half lamb
- ½ sliced onion
- garlic cloves minced
- tbsp. dried dill
- tsp salt
- ½ tsp black pepper

Directions:

1. Blend the ingredients gently in a large bowl until well combined. Overworking the meat will cause it to be tough.
2. Form the meat into burgers.
3. Grill or fry in a pan on medium-high heat until cooked through, 4-5 min per side. If preparing in a pan, to sear both sides quickly, then throw the burgers in a 350° F oven for 10 min to finish cooking through.
4. Serve with Tzatziki for dipping!

Nutrition: Calories: 207 kcal Protein: 22.68 g Fat: 11.89 g Carbohydrates: 1.17 g

Tandoori Lamb Tail

Preparation Time: 10 minutes

Cooking Time: 1hour and 10 minutes

Servings: 2-4

Ingredients:

- Roast meat
- lb. minced lamb
- diced onion
- 5 finely chopped garlic cloves
- serrano pepper, chopped
- 5 tbsp. organic tomato puree
- tsp bell pepper
- tsp coriander powder
- tsp turmeric
- tsp salt
- ¼ tsp freshly ground black pepper
- ¼ tsp cumin powder
- ¼ tsp ground cloves
- ¼ tsp cinnamon (ground)
- A pinch freshly grated nutmeg
- eggs
- A small hand of chopped mint
- "Ketchup" filling
- 5 tbsp. organic tomato puree
- ¼ cup water
- A pinch of salt and pepper
- A pinch of garlic powder

Directions:

1. Bring all the ingredients in a bowl, then mix and divide the mixture into a bowl with greased bread.
2. Bake the bread at 350° C for 1 hour.
3. While the bread is baking, prepare the tomato sauce by mixing the ingredients in a pan over low heat.
4. When the bread is ready, apply ketchup and put it in the oven for 10 minutes.
5. Take off from the oven, then let stand for a few minutes to cool the juice, remove the meatloaf from the pan, and serve.

Nutrition: Calories: 506 kcal Protein: 45.93 g Fat: 30.01 g Carbohydrates: 11.82 g

POULTRY

Buffalo Pizza Chicken

Preparation Time: 5 minutes

Cooking Time: 5-6 minutes

Servings: 5

Ingredients:

- Vegetable cooking spray
- ½ cup Buffalo-style hot sauce
- (16-oz) package prebaked Italian pizza crust
- cups chopped deli-roasted whole chicken
- cup (4 oz) shredded Provolone cheese
- ¼ cup crumbled blue cheese

Directions:

1. Coat the grill with the spray and put it on the grill. Preheat grill to 350° F (medium heat).
2. Spread the hot sauce over the crust, and the next 3 ingredients surface.
3. Place the crust on the cooking grate directly. Grill at 350° F (medium heat) for 4 min, covered with the grill lid.
4. Rotate 1-quarter turn pizza and grill, covered with grill top, for 5 to 6 min or until heated thoroughly. Serve right away.

Nutrition: Calories: 365 Fat,: 11g Net Carbs: 42g Protein: 24g

Hot Chicken Meatballs

Preparation Time: 5 minutes

Cooking Time: 21 minutes

Servings: 2

Ingredients:

- pound ground chicken
- Salt and black pepper, to taste
- tablespoons yellow mustard
- ½ cup almond flour
- ¼ cup mozzarella cheese, grated
- ¼ cup hot sauce
- egg

Directions:

1. Preheat oven to 4000F and line a baking tray with parchment paper.
2. In a bowl, combine the chicken, black pepper, mustard, flour, mozzarella cheese, salt, and egg. Form meatballs and arrange them on the baking tray.
3. Cook for 16 minutes, then pour over the hot sauce and bake for 5 more minutes.

Nutrition: Calories: 487 Fat,: 35g Net Carbs: 4.3g, Protein: 31.5g

Intermittent Chicken Enchaladas

Preparation Time: 10 minutes

Cooking Time: 25 minutes

Servings: 6

Ingredients:

- 2 cups gluten-free enchilada sauce
- Chicken
- tablespoon Avocado oil
- 4 cloves Garlic (minced)
- cups Shredded chicken (cooked)
- ¼ cup Chicken broth
- ¼ cup fresh cilantro (chopped)
- Assembly
- 12 Coconut tortillas
- 3/4 cup Colby jack cheese (shredded)
- ¼ cup Green onions (chopped)

Direction:

1. Warm oil at medium to high heat in a large pan. Add the chopped garlic and cook until fragrant for about a minute.
2. Add rice, 1 cup enchilada sauce (half the total), chicken, and coriander. Simmer for 5 minutes.
3. In the meantime, heat the oven to 3750 F. Grease a 9x13 baking dish.
4. In the middle of each tortilla, place ¼ cup chicken mixture. Roll up and place seam side down in the baking dish.
5. Pour the remaining cup enchilada sauce over the enchiladas. Sprinkle with shredded cheese.

---

6. Bake for 10 to 12 minutes Sprinkle with green onions.

Nutrition: Calories: 349 Fat,: 19g Net Carbs: 9g Protein: 31g

Home-Style Chicken Kebab

Preparation Time: 10 minutes

Cooking Time: 10 minutes

Servings: 2

Ingredients:

- 2 Roma tomatoes, chopped
- pound chicken thighs, boneless, skinless and halved
- tablespoons olive oil
- 1/2 cup Greek-style yogurt
- ½ ounce Swiss cheese, sliced

Directions:

1. Place the chicken thighs, yogurt, tomatoes, and olive oil in a glass storage container. You can add in mustard seeds, cinnamon, and sumac if desired.
2. Cover then place in the fridge to marinate for 3 to 4 hours.
3. Thread the chicken thighs onto skewers, creating a thick log shape. Grill the kebabs over medium-high heat for 3 or 4 minutes on each side.
4. Use an instant-read thermometer to check the doneness of meat; it should read about 165 degrees F.
5. Top with the cheese; continue to cook for 4 minutes or until cheesy is melted. Enjoy!

Nutrition: 498 Calories 23.2g Fat 6.2g Carbs 61g Protein 1.7g Fiber

SEAFOOD RECIPES

Low Carb Soft Shell Crab

Preparation time: 8 minutes

Cooking time: 8 minutes

Servings: 2

Ingredients:

- 2 eggs
- Soft shell crabs (8)
- Powdered (½ cup)
- Carolina BBQ sauce (4 tbsp)

Directions:

1. Shred your parmesan until it's smooth then set it aside.
2. Beat your eggs and set aside.
3. Heat a large pan with half cup of lard to medium heat. Dry the crab with a paper towel.
4. Pour the parmesan into a shallow dish.
5. Pour your eggs into another shallow dish.
6. Dip each crab in the egg dish very lightly then dip the egg coated crab into the Parmesan dish and coat heavily.
7. Fry the crabs in hot oil for about 2 minutes. Flip occasionally until the whole crab is thoroughly cooked.
8. Serve fresh with Carolina BBQ sauce

Nutrition: 2 servings contain 388 calories Fats: 14g Protein: 16g Carbs: 2g Fiber: 1g

Cheese and Seafood Stuffed Mushrooms

Preparation time: 10 minutes

Cooking time: 55 minutes

Servings: 30

Ingredients:

- Paleo mayo (¼ cup)
- Chopped cooked shrimp (1 cup)
- Cream cheese (¾ package)
- Drained crab meat (1 can)
- Parmesan cheese. Grated. (¼ cup)
- Onion powder (½ teaspoon)
- Dijon mustard (1 teaspoon)
- Garlic powder (¼ teaspoon)
- Sharp cheddar cheese. Grated (½ cup)
- Chopped parsley (1 tablespoon)
- Clean large white button mushrooms (36)
- Frank's red hot (This is optional)

Directions:

1. Using parchment paper, line a fairly sized baking sheet
2. Mix all the ingredients except the mushrooms in a mixing bowl and stir gently.
3. Hold the mushrooms in one hand and use a spoon in the other hand to fill the mushroom holes with the mixed ingredients. Put just enough filling to create a tiny mountain on your mushroom.
4. Arrange the stuffed mushrooms on the lined baking sheet and put the sheet in the fridge for about 30 minutes.

5. While that's going on, prep your oven to 375°F.
6. After 30 minutes, transfer the baking sheet to the oven and leave until it looks brownish. This should take about 20 minutes.
7. Remove them from the oven and let them cool for 5 minutes before sprinkling with parsley.
8. Serve.

Nutrition: 1 serving contains 49 calories Fats: 3.0g Carbs: 1.4g Protein: 4.0g

Intermittent Salmon in Foil Packets With Pesto

Preparation time: 10 minutes

Cooking time: 20 minutes

Servings: 4

Ingredients:

- Tomatoes (20)
- Salmon fillet (1 pound)
- Kosher salt (½ tsp)
- Dry white wine (½ cup)
- Olive oil(2 tbsp)
- Ground black pepper (⅛ tsp)
- Basil pesto (¼ cup)
- Cauliflower rice (optional)

Directions:

1. Put the salmon on a very large tin foil.
2. Sprinkle some salt and pepper.
3. Drizzle a bit of olive oil
4. Arrange the cherry tomatoes around the fish then fold up the foil in such a way that it resembles a mini volcano.
5. Drizzle the white wine over the salmon through the tiny hole at the top.
6. Now seal the top of your volcano and cook on a grill at about 400°F for 10 minutes.
7. Take it out of the grill but leave it sealed for 5 minutes.
8. Open it and glaze the salmon with pesto.
9. Serve with cauliflower rice if you like.
10. Enjoy!

Nutrition: 4 servings contain 393 calories. Fat: 29g Carbs: 4g Protein: 27g Fiber: 1g

Simple Founder in Brown Butter Lemon Sauce

Preparation Time: 10 minutes

Cooking Time: 10 minutes

Servings: 4

Ingredients:

- For the Sauce:
- ½ cup unsalted grass-fed butter, cut into pieces
- Juice of 1 lemon
- Sea salt, for seasoning
- Freshly ground black pepper, for seasoning
- For the Fish:
- 4 (4-ounce) boneless flounder fillets
- Sea salt, for seasoning
- Freshly ground black pepper, for seasoning
- ¼ cup almond flour
- 2 tablespoons good-quality olive oil
- tablespoon chopped fresh parsley

Directions:

1. To make the Sauce:
2. Brown the butter. In a medium saucepan at medium heat, cook the butter, stirring it once in a while, until it is golden brown, at least 4 minutes.
3. Finish the sauce. Remove the saucepan from the heat and stir in the lemon juice. Spice the sauce with salt and pepper and set it aside.
4. To make a Fish:Season the fish. Pat the fish fillets dry then spice them lightly with salt and pepper. Spoon the

almond flour onto a plate, then roll the fish fillets through the flour until they are lightly coated. Cook the fish. In a large skillet at medium-high heat, warm the olive oil. Add the fish fillets and fry them until they are crispy and golden on both sides, 2 to 3 minutes per side.
Serve. Moved the fish to a serving plate and drizzle with the sauce. Top with the parsley and serve it hot.

Nutrition: Calories: 389 Total fat: 33g Total carbs: 1g Fiber: 0g Net carbs: 1g Sodium: 256mg Protein: 22g

Grilled Calamari

Preparation Time: 10 minutes

Cooking Time: 5 minutes

Servings: 4

Ingredients:

- 2 pounds calamari tubes and tentacles, cleaned
- ½ cup good-quality olive oil
- Zest and juice of 2 lemons
- 2 tablespoons chopped fresh oregano
- tablespoon minced garlic
- ¼ teaspoon sea salt
- ⅛ teaspoon freshly ground black pepper

Directions:

1. Prepare the calamari. Score the top layer of the calamari tubes about 2 inches apart.
2. Marinate the calamari. In a large bowl, stir together the olive oil, lemon zest, lemon juice, oregano, garlic, salt, and pepper. Add the calamari and toss to coat it well, then place it in the refrigerator to marinate for at least 30 minutes to 1 hour. Grill the calamari. Preheat a grill to high heat. Grill the calamari, turning once, for about 3 minutes total, until it's tender and lightly charred.
3. Serve. Divide the calamari between four plates and serve it hot.

Nutrition: Calories: 455 Total fat: 30g Total carbs: 8g Fiber: 1g; Net carbs: 7g Sodium: 101mg Protein: 35g

Souvlaki Spiced Salmon Bowls

Preparation Time: 10 minutes

Cooking Time: 20 minutes

Servings: 4

Ingredients:

- For the Salmon:
- ¼ cup good-quality olive oil
- Juice of 1 lemon
- 2 tablespoons chopped fresh oregano
- tablespoon minced garlic
- tablespoon balsamic vinegar
- tablespoon smoked sweet paprika
- ½ teaspoon sea salt
- ¼ teaspoon freshly ground black pepper
- 4 (4-ounce) salmon fillets

Directions:

1. To make the Salmon:
2. Marinate the fish. In a medium bowl, put and mix the olive oil, lemon juice, oregano, garlic, vinegar, paprika, salt, and pepper. Put the salmon and turn to coat it well with the marinade. Cover the bowl and let the salmon sit marinating for 15 to 20 minutes.
3. Grill the fish. Preheat the grill to medium-high heat and grill the fish until just cooked through, 4 to 5 minutes per side. Set the fish aside on a plate.
4. For the Bowls:
5. 2 tablespoons good-quality olive oil
6. red bell pepper, cut into strips
7. yellow bell pepper, cut into strips

8. zucchini, cut into ½-inch strips lengthwise
9. cucumber, diced
10. large tomato, chopped
11. ½ cup sliced Kalamata olives
12. 6 ounces feta cheese, crumbled
13. ½ cup sour cream

Nutrition: Calories: 553 Total fat: 44g Total carbs: 10g Fiber: 3g; Net carbs: 7g Sodium: 531mg Protein: 30g

Proscuitto-Wrapped Haddock

Preparation Time: 10 minutes

Cooking Time: 15 minutes

Servings: 4

Ingredients:

- 4 (4-ounce) haddock fillets, about 1 inch thick
- Sea salt, for seasoning
- Freshly ground black pepper, for seasoning
- 4 slices prosciutto (2 ounces)
- 3 tablespoons garlic-infused olive oil
- Juice and zest of 1 lemon

Directions:

1. Preheat the oven. Set the oven temperature to 350°F. Line a baking sheet with parchment paper.
2. Prepare the fish. Pat the fish dry using paper towels then spice it lightly on both sides with salt and pepper. Wrap the prosciutto around the fish tightly but carefully so it doesn't rip.
3. Bake the fish. Bring the fish on the baking sheet and drizzle it with the olive oil. Bake for 15 to 17 minutes until the fish flakes easily with a fork.
4. Serve. Divide the fish between four plates and top with the lemon zest and a drizzle of lemon juice.

Nutrition: Calories: 282 Total fat: 18g Total carbs: 1g Fiber: 0g; Net carbs: 1g Sodium: 76mg Protein: 29g

Grilled Salmon with Caponata

Preparation Time: 15 minutes

Cooking Time: 20 minutes

Servings: 4

Ingredients:

- ¼ cup good-quality olive oil, divided
- onion, chopped
- celery stalks, chopped
- tablespoon minced garlic
- tomatoes, chopped
- ½ cup chopped marinated artichoke hearts
- ¼ cup pitted green olives, chopped
- ¼ cup cider vinegar
- tablespoons white wine
- tablespoons chopped pecans
- (4-ounce) salmon fillets
- Freshly ground black pepper, for seasoning
- 2 tablespoons chopped fresh basil

Directions:

1. Make the caponata. In a large skillet at medium heat, warm 3 tablespoons of the olive oil. Add the onion, celery, garlic, and sauté until they have softened, about 4 minutes. Stir in the tomatoes, artichoke hearts, olives, vinegar, white wine, and pecans. Place the mixture to a boil, then reduce the heat to low and simmer until the liquid has reduced, 6 to 7 minutes. Take off the skillet from the heat and set it aside.
2. Grill the fish. Preheat a grill to medium-high heat. Pat the fish dry using paper towels then rub it with the

remaining 1 tablespoon of olive oil and season lightly with black pepper. Grill the salmon, turning once, until it is just cooked through, about 8 minutes total.

3. Serve. Divide the salmon between four plates, top with a generous scoop of the caponata, and serve immediately with fresh basil.

Nutrition: Calories: 348 Total fat: 25g Total carbs: 7g Fiber: 3g Net carbs: 4g Sodium: 128mg Protein: 24g

Sweet Crab Cakes

Preparation Time: 15 minutes

Cooking Time: 10 minutes

Servings: 4

Ingredients:

- pound cooked lump crabmeat, drained and picked over
- ¼ cup shredded unsweetened coconut
- tablespoon Dijon mustard
- scallion, finely chopped
- ¼ cup minced red bell pepper
- egg, lightly beaten
- teaspoon lemon zest
- Pinch cayenne pepper
- tablespoons coconut flour
- tablespoons coconut oil
- ¼ cup Classic Aioli

Directions:

1. Make the crab cakes. In a medium bowl, mix the crab, coconut, mustard, scallion, red bell pepper, egg, lemon zest, and cayenne until it holds together. Form the mixture into eight equal patties about ¾ inch thick.
2. Chill. Place the patties on a plate, cover the plate with plastic wrap, and chill them in the refrigerator for around 1 hour to 12 hours.
3. Coat the patties. Spread the coconut flour on a plate. Dip each patty in the flour until it is lightly coated.
4. Cook. In a large skillet at medium heat, warm the coconut oil. Fry the crab-cake patties, turning them once,

until they are golden and cooked through, about 5 minutes per side.

5. Serve. Place two crab cakes on each of four plates and serve with the aioli.

Nutrition: Calories: 370 Total fat: 24g Total carbs: 12g Fiber: 6g Net carbs: 6g Sodium: 652mg Protein: 26g

VEGETABLES

Spinach and Eggs Scramble

Preparation time: 5 minutes

Cooking time: 10 minutes

Servings: 2

Ingredients:

- 4 oz spinach
- ¼ tsp salt
- 1/8 tsp ground black pepper
- tbsp unsalted butter
- eggs, beaten

Directions:

1. Take a frying pan, place it over medium heat, add butter and when it melts, add spinach and cook for 5 minutes until leaves have wilted.
2. Then pour in eggs, season with salt and black pepper, and cook for 3 minutes until eggs have scramble to the desired level.
3. Serve.

Nutrition: 90 Calories; 7 g Fats; 5.6 g Protein; 0.7 g Net Carb; 0.6 g Fiber;

Breakfast Burgers with Avocado

Preparation time: 5 minutes

Cooking time: 15 minutes

Servings: 2

Ingredients:

- 4 strips of bacon
- 2 tbsp chopped lettuce
- 2 avocados
- 2 eggs
- 2 tbsp mayonnaise
- Seasoning:
- ¼ tsp salt
- ¼ tsp sesame seeds

Directions:

1. Take a skillet pan, place it over medium heat and when hot, add bacon strips and cook for 5 minutes until crispy.
2. Transfer bacon to a plate lined with paper towels, crack an egg into the pan, and cook for 2 to 4 minutes or until fried to the desired level; fry remaining egg in the same manner.
3. Prepare sandwiches and for this, cut each avocado in half widthwise, remove the pit, and scoop out the flesh.
4. Fill the hollow of two avocado halves with mayonnaise, then top each half with 1 tbsp of chopped lettuce, 2 bacon strips, and a fried egg, and then cover with the second half of avocado.
5. Sprinkle sesame seeds on avocados and serve.

Nutrition: 205.2 Calories; 18.5 g Fats; 7.7 g Protein; 0.7 g Net Carb; 1.9 g Fiber;

Zucchini and Broccoli Fritters

Preparation time: 10 minutes

Cooking time: 10 minutes

Servings: 2

Ingredients:

- ounce chopped broccoli
- zucchini, grated, squeezed
- eggs
- tbsp almond flour
- ½ tsp nutritional yeast
- Seasoning:
- 1/3 tsp salt
- ¼ tsp dried basil
- tbsp avocado oil

Directions:

1. Wrap grated zucchini in a cheesecloth, twist it well to remove excess moisture, and then place zucchini in a bowl.
2. Add remaining Ingredients, except for oil, and then whisk well until combined.
3. Take a skillet pan, place it over medium heat, add oil and when hot, drop zucchini mixture in four portions, shape them into flat patties and cook for 4 minutes per side until thoroughly cooked.
4. Serve.

Nutrition: 191 Calories; 16.6 g Fats; 9.6 g Protein; 0.8 g Net Carb; 0.2 g Fiber;

Vegetable Greek Mousaka

Preparation Time: 10 minutes

Cooking Time: 40 minutes

Servings: 6

Ingredients:

- 2 large eggplants, cut into strips
- cup diced celery
- cup diced carrots
- small white onion, chopped
- eggs
- tsp olive oil
- cups grated Parmesan
- cup ricotta cheese
- cloves garlic, minced
- tsp Italian seasoning blend
- Salt to taste
- Sauce:
- ½ cups heavy cream
- ¼ cup butter, melted
- cup grated mozzarella cheese
- tsp Italian seasoning
- ¾ cup almond flour

Directions:

1. Preheat the oven to 350°F. Put the eggplant strips on a paper towel, sprinkle with salt, and let sit there to exude liquid. Heat olive oil in a skillet over medium heat and sauté the onion, celery, and carrots for 5 minutes. Stir in

the garlic and cook further for 30 seconds; set aside to cool.

2. Mix the eggs, 1 cup of Parmesan cheese, ricotta cheese, and salt in a bowl; set aside. Pour the heavy cream in a pot and bring to heat over a medium fire while continually stirring. Stir in the remaining Parmesan cheese, and 1 teaspoon of Italian seasoning. Turn the heat off and set aside.

3. To lay the mousaka, spread a small amount of the sauce at the bottom of the baking dish. Pat dry the eggplant strips and make a single layer on the sauce. Put a layer of ricotta cheese on the eggplants, sprinkle some veggies on it, and repeat the layering process until all the ingredients are exhausted.

4. In a small bowl, evenly mix the melted butter, almond flour, and 1 teaspoon of Italian seasoning. Spread the top of the mousaka layers with it and sprinkle the top with mozzarella cheese. Cover the dish using foil and place it in the oven to bake for 25 minutes. Take off the foil then bake for at least 5 minutes until the cheese is slightly burned. Slice the mousaka and serve warm.

Nutrition: Calories: 476 Fat 35g Net Carbs 9.6g Protein 33g

SOUPS AND STEWS

Veggie Beef Soup

Preparation Time: 10 minutes

Cooking Time: 0 minutes

Servings: 6

Ingredients:

- 6 cups beef broth
- cup heavy cream
- pound lean ground beef
- cup frozen mixed vegetables
- yellow onion, chopped
- Salt & black pepper, to taste

Directions:

1. Add all the ingredients minus the salt, black pepper and heavy cream and bring to a boil. Reduce the heat to a simmer and cook for 40 minutes.
2. Before the soup is done cooking, warm the heavy cream, and then add once the soup is cooked.
3. Season with salt and black pepper and serve.

Nutrition: Calories: 270 Carbs: 6g Fiber: 2g Net Carbs: 4g Fat: 14g Protein: 29g

Pumpkin Kale Vegetarian Stew

Preparation Time: 10 minutes

Cooking Time: 40 minutes

Servings: 6

Ingredients:

- 4 cups vegetable broth
- cup pumpkin, cubed
- carrots, chopped
- yellow onion, chopped
- cloves garlic, chopped
- cup kale, chopped
- Salt & black pepper, to taste

Directions:

1. Add all the ingredients minus the salt and black pepper to a stockpot and bring to a boil. Reduce heat to a simmer and cook for 40 minutes.
2. Season with salt and black pepper and serve.

Nutrition: Calories: 62 Carbs: 9g Fiber: 2g Net Carbs: 7g Fat: 1g Protein: 4g

Lime-Mint Soup

Preparation Time: 5 minutes

Cooking Time: 20 minutes

Servings: 4

Ingredients:

- 4 cups vegetable broth
- ¼ cup fresh mint leaves, roughly chopped
- ¼ cup chopped scallions, white and green parts
- 3 garlic cloves, minced
- 3 tablespoons freshly squeezed lime juice

Directions:

1. In a large stockpot, combine the broth, mint, scallions, garlic, and lime juice. Bring to a boil over medium-high heat.
2. Cover, reduce the heat to low, simmer for 15 minutes, and serve.

Nutrition: Calories: 55 Total fat: 2g Carbohydrates: 5g Fiber: 1g Protein: 5g

Cheesy Cauliflower Soup

Preparation Time: 10 minutes

Cooking Time: 30 minutes

Servings: 8

Ingredients:

- ¼ cup butter
- 1 head cauliflower, chopped
- ½ onion, chopped
- ½ teaspoon ground nutmeg
- 4 cups chicken stock
- 1 cup heavy whipping cream
- Salt and freshly ground black pepper, to taste
- 1 cup Cheddar cheese, shredded

Directions:

1. Take a large stockpot and place it over medium heat.
2. Add butter to this pot and let it melt.
3. Add cauliflower and onion to the melted butter and sauté for 10 minutes until these veggies are soft.
4. Add nutmeg and chicken stock to the pot and bring to a boil.
5. Reduce the heat to low and allow it to simmer for 15 minutes.
6. Remove the stockpot from the heat and then add heavy cream.
7. Purée the cooked soup with an immersion blender until smooth.
8. Sprinkle this soup with salt and black pepper.
9. Garnish with Cheddar cheese and serve warm.

Nutrition: Calories: 224 Fat: 16.8g Total carbs: 10.8g Fiber: 2.2g Protein: 9.6g

SNACKS

Peppers and Hummus

Preparation Time: 15 minutes

Cooking Time: 0 minutes

Servings: 4

Ingredients:

- one 15-ounce can chickpeas, drained and rinsed
- juice of 1 lemon, or 1 tablespoon prepared lemon juice
- ¼ cup tahini
- 3 tablespoons olive oil
- ½ teaspoon ground cumin
- tablespoon water
- ¼ teaspoon paprika
- red bell pepper, sliced
- green bell pepper, sliced
- orange bell pepper, sliced

Directions:

1. In a food processor, combine chickpeas, lemon juice, tahini, 2 tablespoons of the olive oil, the cumin, and water.
2. A process on high speed until blended, about 30 seconds. Scoop the hummus into a bowl and drizzle with the remaining tablespoon of olive oil. Sprinkle with paprika and serve with sliced bell peppers.

Nutrition: Calories: 364 kcal Protein: 12.41 g Fat: 22.53 g Carbohydrates: 31.65 g

Deconstructed Hummus Pitas

Preparation Time: 15 minutes

Cooking Time: 0 minutes

Servings: 4

Ingredients:

- garlic clove, crushed
- ¾ cup tahini (sesame paste
- tablespoons fresh lemon juice
- teaspoon salt
- 1⁄8 teaspoon ground cayenne
- 1⁄4 cup water
- 11⁄2 cups cooked or 1 (15.5 oz. can) chickpeas, rinsed and drained
- medium carrots, grated (about 1 cup
- (7-inch pita bread, preferably whole wheat, halved
- large ripe tomato, cut into 1⁄4-inch slices
- cups fresh baby spinach

Directions:

1. In a blender or food processor, mince the garlic. Add the tahini, lemon juice, salt, cayenne, and water. Process until smooth.
2. Take the chickpeas in a bowl and crush slightly with a fork. Add the carrots and the reserved tahini sauce and toss to combine. Set aside.
3. Spoon 2 or 3 tablespoons of the chickpea mixture into each pita half. Tuck a tomato slice and a few spinach leaves into each pocket and serve.

Nutrition: Calories: 885 kcal Protein: 39.5 g Fat: 36.19 g Carbohydrates: 109.52 g

Refried Bean And Salsa Quesadillas

Preparation Time: 5 minutes

Cooking Time: 6 minutes

Servings: 4

Ingredients:

- tablespoon canola oil, plus for frying
- 1½ cups cooked or 1 (15.5 oz. Can) pinto beans, drained and mashed
- teaspoon chili powder
- 4 (10-inch whole-wheat flour tortillas
- cup tomato salsa, homemade or store-bought
- ½ cup minced red onion (optional

Directions:

1. In a medium saucepan, heat the oil at medium heat. Put the mashed beans and chili powder and cook, stirring, until hot, about 5 minutes. Set aside.
2. To make, put 1 tortilla on a work surface and scoop at least ¼ cup of the beans across the bottom.
3. Put on the top the beans with the salsa and onion, if using.
4. Fold the top half of the tortilla on the filling and press slightly.
5. In a large skillet, warm a thin layer of oil over medium heat. Place the folded quesadillas, 1 or 2 at a time, into the hot skillet and heat until hot, turning once, about 1 minute per side.
6. Cut the quesadillas into 3 or 4 then set it on plates.
7. Serve immediately.

Nutrition: Calories: 940 kcal Protein: 55.58 g Fat: 12.07 g
Carbohydrates: 158.5 g

SMOOTHIES AND DRINKS

Strawberry Almond Smoothie

Preparation Time: 10 minutes

Cooking Time: 0 minutes

Servings: 2

Ingredients:

- .25 cup Frozen unsweetened strawberries
- 2 tbsp. Whey vanilla isolate powder
- .5 cup Heavy cream
- 16 oz. Unsweetened almond milk
- Stevia (as desired)

Directions:

1. Toss or pour each of the fixings into a blender.
2. Puree until smooth.
3. Pour a small amount of water to thin the smoothie as needed.

Nutrition: Protein Count: 15 grams Total Fat Content: 25 grams Net Carbohydrates: 7 grams Calorie Count: 34

Blueberry Yogurt Smoothie

Preparation Time: 5 minutes

Cooking Time: 0 minutes

Servings: 2

Ingredients:

- 10 Blueberries
- cup Coconut milk
- Stevia (to taste)

Directions:

1. Combine all of the fixings in the blender. Mix well.
2. When creamy, pour into two chilled glasses and enjoy.

Nutrition: Protein Count: 2 grams Total Fat Content: 5 grams Net Carbohydrates: 2 grams Calorie Count: 70

DESSERTS

Quick and Simple Brownie

Preparation Time: 20 minutes

Cooking Time: 5 minutes

Servings: 2

Ingredients:

- 3 Tbsp. Intermittent chocolate chips
- Tbsp. unsweetened cacao powder
- Tbsp. salted butter
- 2¼ Tbsp. powdered sugar

Directions:

1. Combine 2 tbsp. of chocolate chips and butter, melt them in a microwave for 10-15 minutes. Add the remaining chocolate chips, stir and make a sauce.
2. Add the cacao powder and powdered sugar to the sauce and whisk well until you have a dough.
3. Place the dough on a baking sheet, form the Brownie.
4. Put your Brownie into the oven (preheated to 350°F).
5. Bake for 5 minutes.

Nutrition: Carbohydrates – 9 g Fat – 30 g Protein – 13 g Calories – 100

Cute Peanut Balls

Preparation Time: 20 minutes

Cooking Time: 20 minutes

Servings: 18

Ingredients:

- cup salted peanuts, chopped
- cup peanut butter
- cup powdered sweetener
- 8 oz intermittent chocolate chips

Directions:

1. Combine the chopped peanuts, peanut butter, and sweetener in a separate dish. Stir well and make a dough. Divide it into 18 pieces and form small balls. Put them in the fridge for 10-15 minutes.
2. Use a microwave to melt your chocolate chips.
3. Plunge each ball into the melted chocolate.
4. Return your balls in the fridge. Cool for about 20 minutes.

Nutrition: Carbohydrates – 7 g Fat – 17 g Protein – 7 g Calories – 194

Chocolate Mug Muffins

Preparation Time: 5 minutes

Cooking Time: 2 minutes

Servings: 4

Ingredients:

- 4 tbsps. almond flour
- tsp baking powder
- 4 tbsp. granulated Erythritol
- tbsp. cocoa powder
- ½ tsp vanilla extract
- pinches salt
- 2 eggs beaten
- tbsp. butter, melted
- tsp coconut oil, for greasing the mug
- ½ oz. sugar-free dark chocolate, chopped

Directions:

1. Mix the dry ingredients together in a separate bowl. Add the melted butter, beaten eggs, and chocolate to the bowl. Stir thoroughly.
2. Divide your dough into 4 pieces. Put these pieces in the greased mugs and put them in the microwave. Cook for 1-1.5 minutes (700 watts).
3. Let them cool for 1 minute and serve.

Nutrition: Carbohydrates – 2 g Fat – 19 g Protein – 5 g Calories – 208

CPSIA information can be obtained
at www.ICGtesting.com
Printed in the USA
BVHW011019220421
605295BV00035B/445

9 781802 331585